VINTAGE FABRIC ACCESSORIES

STYLISH CREATIONS FROM RECYCLED FABRICS

KAORU ISHIKAWA

I always use these two files for meetings with clients. These are a kind of sample book, consisting of pieces of fabric that I used for my main works. The gourd pattern piece that appears on the front cover was from my grandmother's kimono. One day I made a bag from this fabric just for fun; this was my first step as a bag designer.

It has now become my life work to create items using vintage fabrics from Japan and elsewhere. I find most of the fabrics at flea markets and use those that are given to me as well. I select the fabrics I like without being particular about their age or place of origin. I select following my instinct, and enjoy the process of my favourite old fabrics being transformed into new items. I will be delighted if this book inspires people who want to alter old fabrics or make some small items with odd pieces of fabric.

CONTENTS

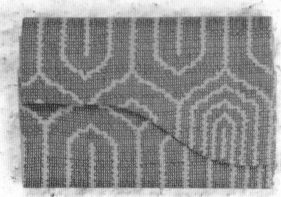

Seal cases (p. 40)/Business card cases (p. 40)

Coasters (p. 41)/Covered buttons (p. 40)

Small coin purses (p. 40)

Notebook covers (p. 41)/Pencil/pen cases (p. 41)

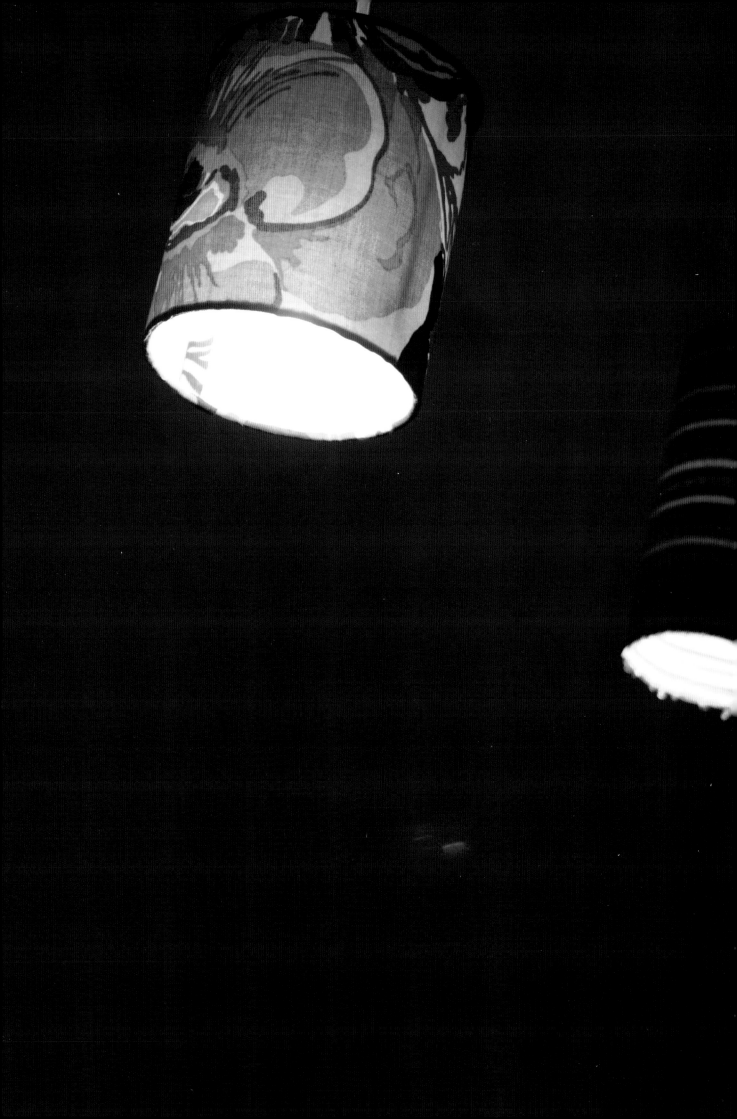

Multi-bags (p. 42)

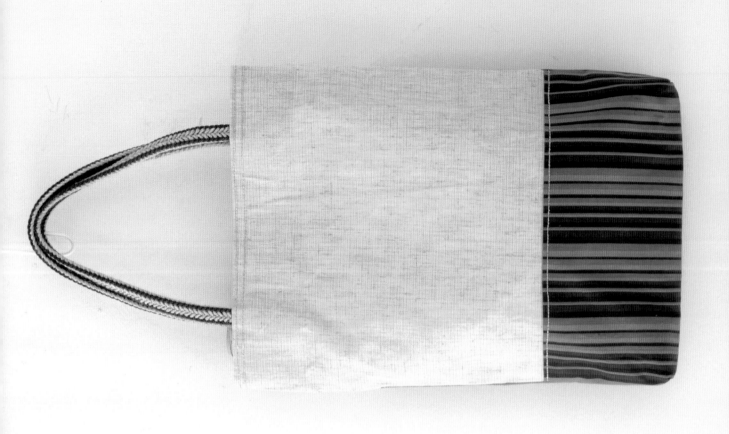

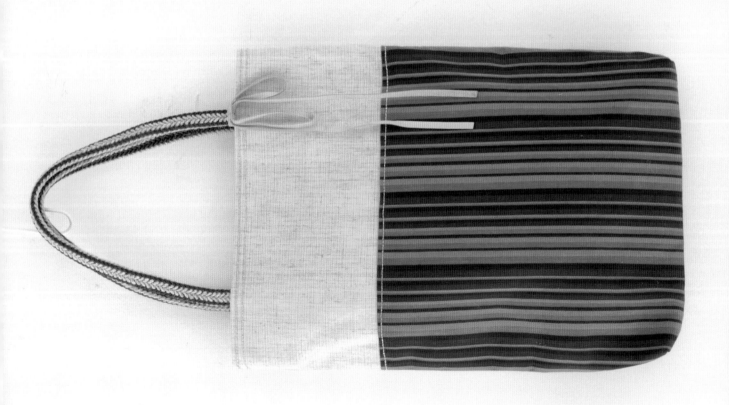

Double-sided bags (p. 42)

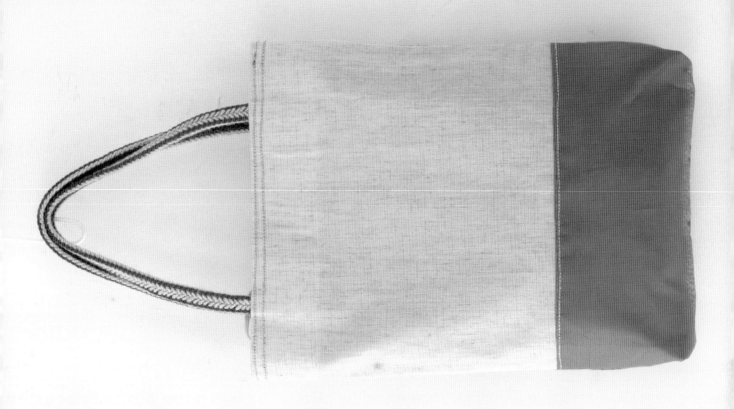

Square bags (p. 43)

Tote bags using obi fabric (p. 42)

Little bird bags (p. 42)

Party purse with chain/clutch purse (p. 43)

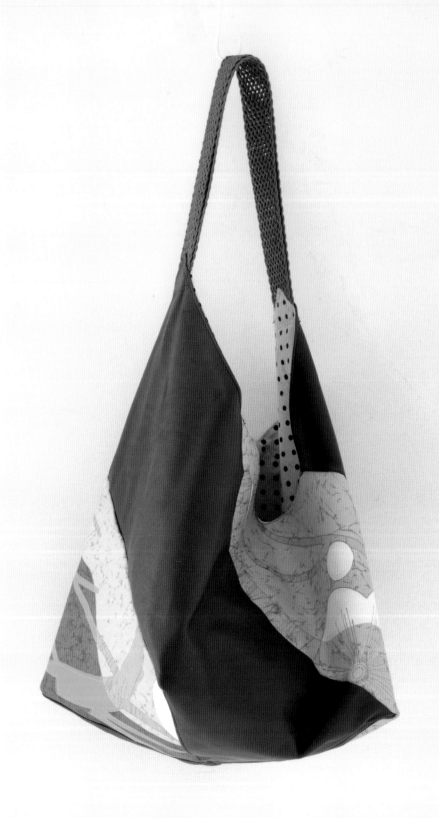

Leather/fabric combination bag (p. 43)

Life of fabric

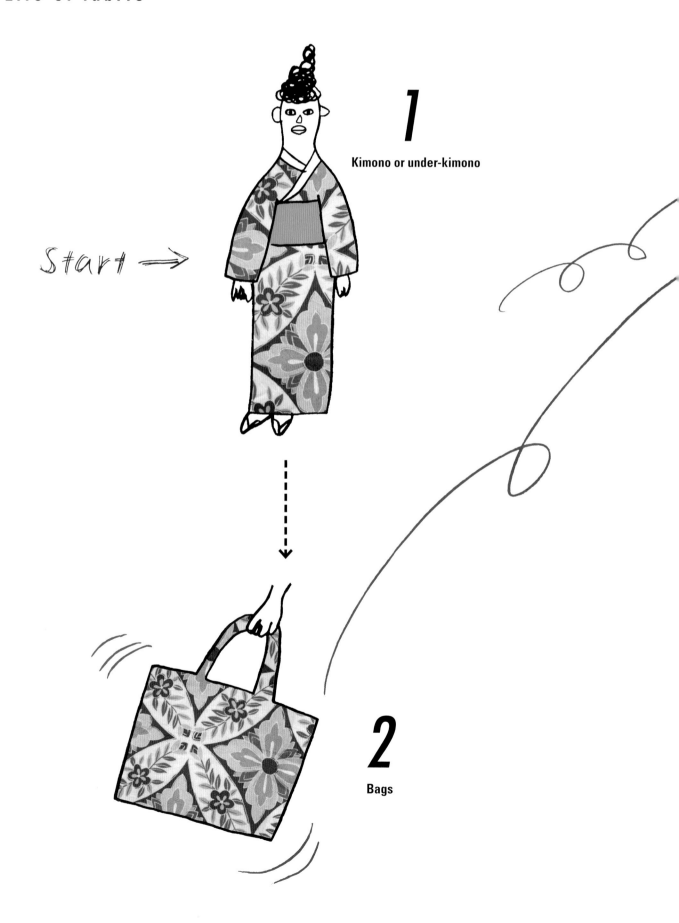

Start ⟹

1
Kimono or under-kimono

2
Bags

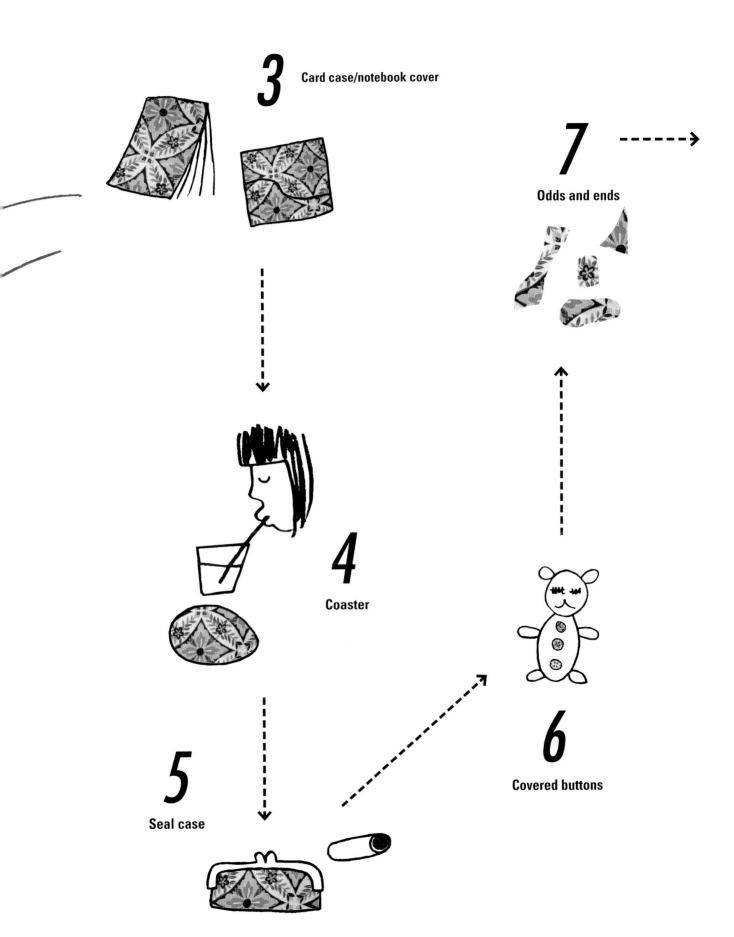

3 Card case/notebook cover

7 Odds and ends

4 Coaster

5 Seal case

6 Covered buttons

Cloth Pieces

What can we make with them?
A lot of things!

---> **Playing with odds and ends**

Buttons and Charms

Combine them with antique buttons and charms

Varieties of Motifs...
CUTE!

Cut out attractive motifs

Ribbons, Laces, and more

Add ribbons and lace

I sometimes affix tiny odd pieces of fabric to letters
to friends. They add a fun, personal touch.
I have also used them as a collage on direct mail.

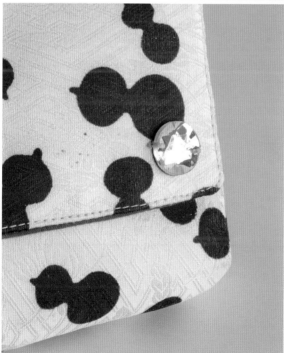

Selecting ornaments is fun

I make a habit of collecting materials such as lace, buttons and charms that might accentuate my pieces. Looking at my collection, I see that I tend to go for old items with antique charm.

1. Cut-out lace used as an applique
2. 1950s vintage ornaments
3. A pompom adds a trendy look
4. Tassel with a Japanese touch
5. Piece of lace bought at a flea market
6. Charm with an antique look
7. Large crystal ornament with a striking presence

Exterior fabrics and linings

Linings are essential for bags and purses. It is fun to select the most suitable ones for the main exterior fabrics. I sometimes use kimono or other vintage fabrics also for the lining, but you can use old shirts, traditional Japanese towels, soft suede material, and more – the choices are unlimited.

Sometimes a pattern you do not think suitable at first may create a great combination, creating a fun surprise for the person who opens the purse.

INDEX

Seal cases (Instructions on p. 65) [left four: kimono fabric/right four: western-pattern vintage fabric]
Good also for storing small jewellery. Choose your favourite pattern for your precious items.

  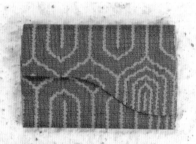

Business card cases (Instructions on p. 62) [left three: kimono fabric/far right: western-pattern vintage fabric]
The two compartments make it easy to organize your own cards and those of others. The special feature of these cases is the curved flap design.

Small coin purse (Instructions on p. 59) [western-pattern vintage fabric]

This palm-size coin purse is useful also for jewellery or pills when travelling.

Double purse (Instructions on p. 60) [western-pattern vintage fabric]

With two compartments, coins and notes can be kept separately. Also useful for organising business cards and other small items.

Vanity case (Instructions on p. 68) [western-pattern vintage fabric]

The large square shape is perfect for cosmetics. Also good as a bag-in-a-bag.

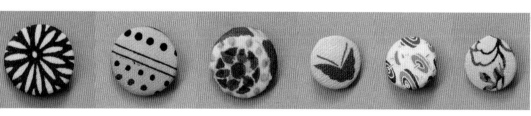 

Covered buttons (Instructions on p. 67) [left six: kimono fabric/right six: western-pattern vintage fabric]
Small odd fabric pieces that are too nice to part with can have a new life as button covering materials. Great on coat or jacket sleeves, or on a simple bag as random highlighting elements.

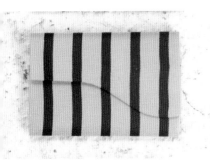

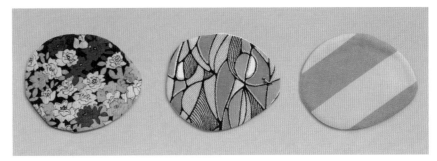

Coasters (Instructions on p. 66) [left two: kimono fabric/far right: western-pattern vintage fabric]
Odd fabric pieces can be transformed into egg-shaped coasters. The imperfect oval is its unique point.

Notebook covers (Instructions on p. 69) [left two: kimono fabric/right two: western-pattern vintage fabric]
Book covers with pen holder made from your favourite fabrics. Dress up simple notebooks.

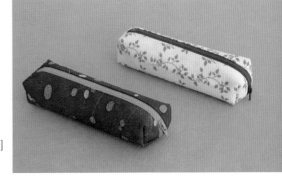

Pencil/pen cases (Instructions on p. 70) [left: kimono fabric/right: western-pattern vintage fabric]
This case has an easy-to-hold slim form and easy-to-open full-length zipper.

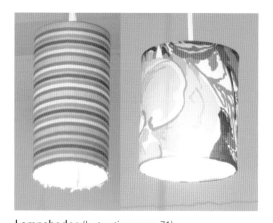 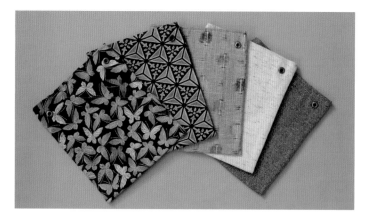

Lampshades (Instructions on p. 71)
[left: obi fabric/right: western-pattern vintage fabric]

The light looks dramatically different depending on the fabric. Unexpected effects can be produced by different fabrics.

Multi-bags (Instructions on p. 72)
[left three: kimono fabric/right two: western-pattern vintage fabric]

By attaching a cord or ribbon through the holes, you can use them as multi-pochettes or tote bags. Have fun by adding as many bags as you like.

Tote bags using obi fabric (Instructions on p. 75)
[obi fabric]

Rigid type bags using attractive obi patterns as they are. The size and shape of this tote make it very versatile.

Double-sided bags (Instructions on p. 73)
[left: kimono fabric/right: western-pattern vintage fabric]

With different fabric combinations between the front and back, this bag has two totally different faces. Choose according to your outfit or your mood.

 Little bird bags (Instructions on p. 76) [left three: kimono fabric/right three: western-pattern vintage fabric]
These single-gusseted bags can become a tote bag or pochette by varying the way the straps are attached. As all types have a little bird motif, they are named 'Little bird' bags.

Square bags (Instructions on p. 74)
[left: obi fabric/right: western-pattern vintage fabric]

With a unique wide handle and large gussets, they are very practical, allowing you to fit a lot in.

City bags (Instructions on p. 81)
[left: kimono fabric/right: western-pattern vintage fabric]

Depending on the combination of different fabrics, the impression changes greatly. These bags are good both with kimono and casual western-style outfits.

Cube bags (Instructions on p. 82) [left: western-pattern vintage fabric/right two: kimono fabric]

The excitement of opening a box inspired this intriguing cubic form. It will add an accent to your fashion.

Party purse with chain/clutch purse
(Instructions on p. 78 – 79) [obi fabric]

Two types of purse, one rounded and one rectangular were made from the same obi fabric and decorated with 1950s vintage ornaments.

Leather/fabric combination bag
(Instructions on p. 80) [western-pattern vintage fabric]

When worn diagonally over one shoulder, it becomes a sling bag. The shape was inspired by an otedama or beanbag used for a traditional Japanese game. The bag is spacious, with a soft, light leather strap. It forms different shapes, depending on what is inside.

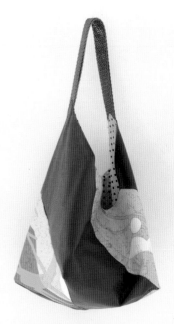

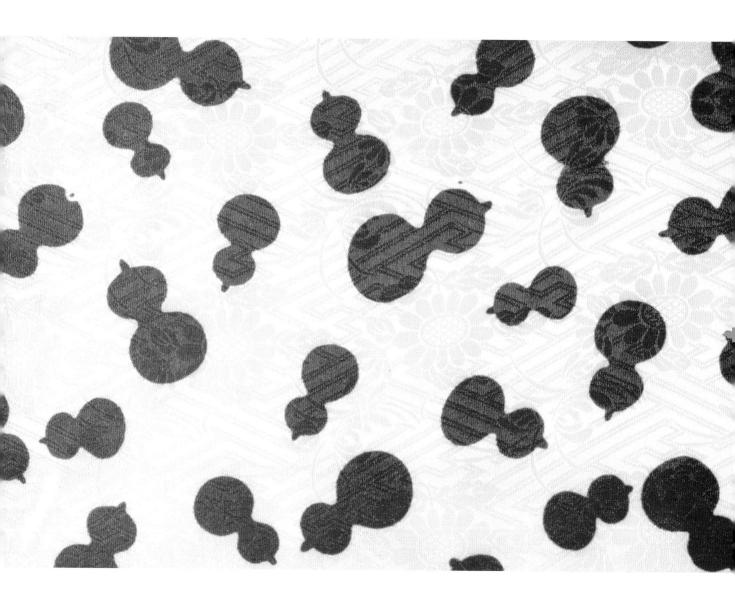

Gourds (Silk)

This fabric was the lining of one of my grandmother's kimonos, made in the late 1920s. It was passed on to my mother and then to me. I like its amusing and brilliant gourd pattern together with the delicate background design.

In addition to its charming appearance, I have a particular emotional attachment to this fabric as it inspired me to become a bag designer.

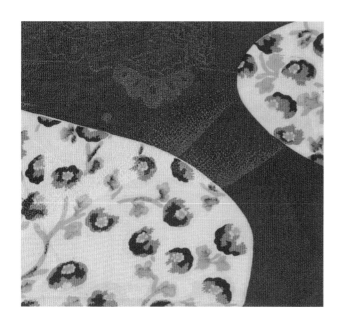

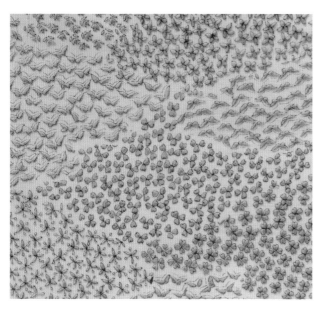

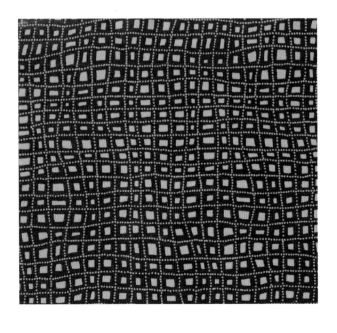

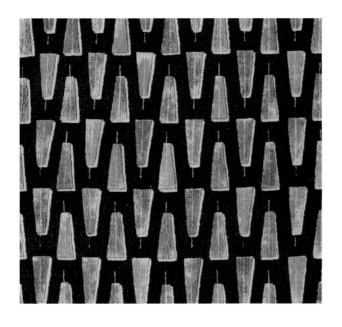

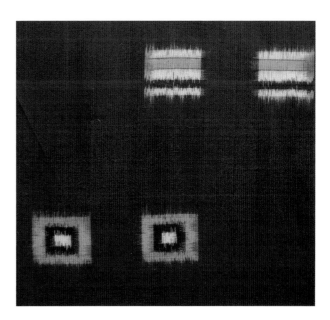

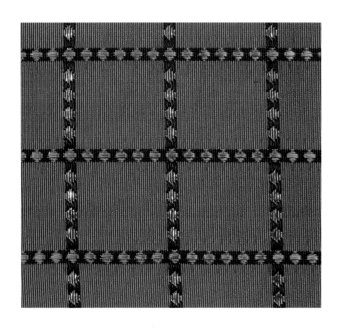
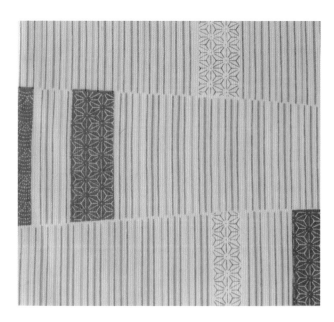

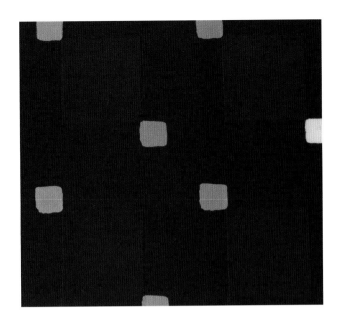

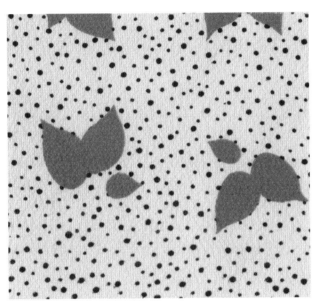
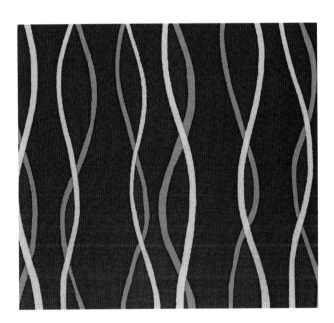
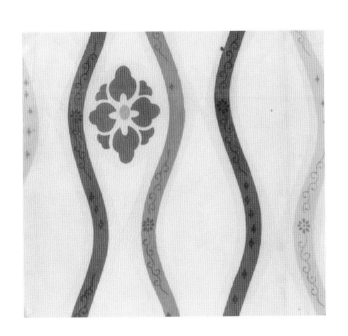
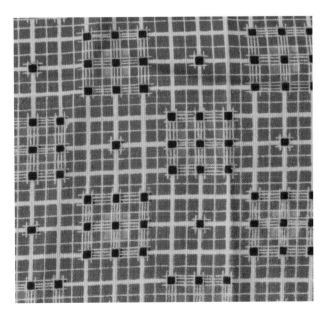

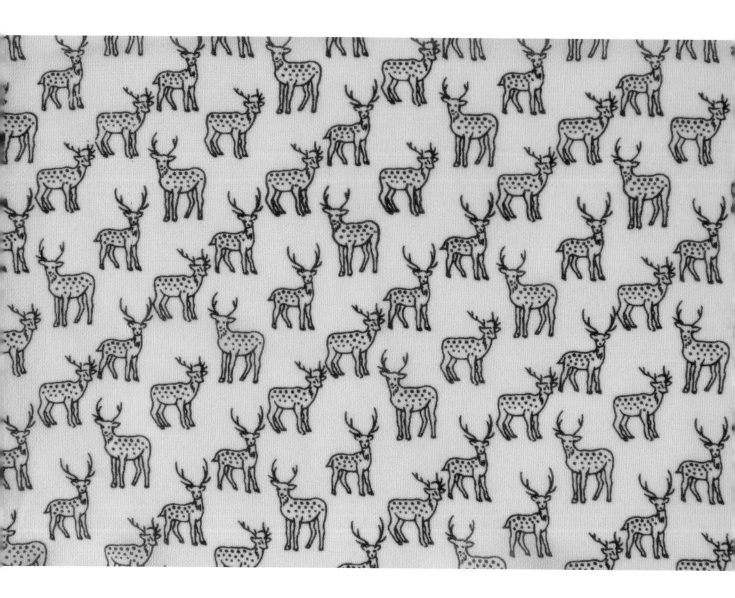

Deer (Synthetic fabric/Japanese)

I found this in a pile of odd pieces at a flea market. As my eyes 'met those of the deer', I did not hesitate to buy it. I am fond of their innocent expression.

Western vintage fabrics are often cotton, but I am not fussy about the material as I select fabrics based on interesting or beautiful patterns and texture.

More attention is required for thin materials, but I like the smooth, pleasant texture of this piece, typical of synthetic materials.

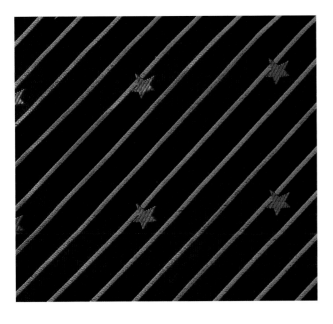
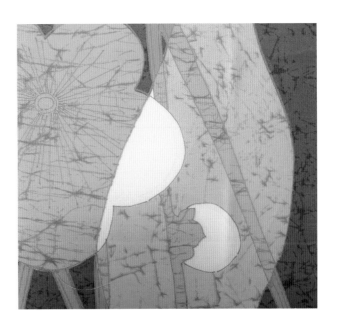

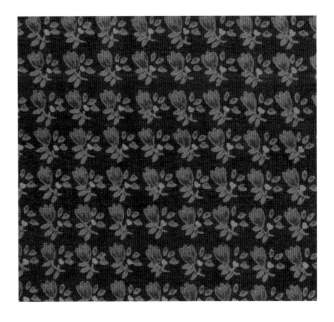

Tools and notions

The tools and notions introduced here are available in handicraft, art supply and large variety stores.

Craft bond

Suitable for fabrics, leather, paper, etc.

Strong industrial bond for purse frames

High-tack adhesives suitable for bags and leather craft.

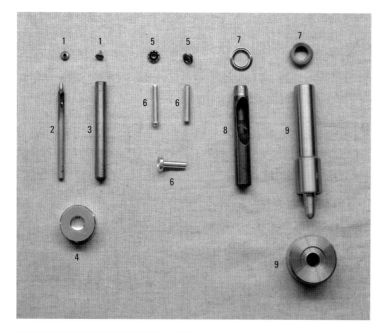

Rivet and eyelet tools

1. Rivets: Metal fittings to fasten leather straps to a bag.
2. Eyelet punch (small): Used to make a small hole in leather. The size varies according to the eyelet and rivet used.
3. Rivet setter: Position on a rivet and tap with a wooden mallet.
4. Anvil: Stand to protect a rivet head from damage
5. Eyelets (small): Reinforcing rings for a hole made for inserting a cord or similar.
6. Eyelet setters (small): Eyelet and setter kits are available. Select the setter according to the size of eyelet.
7. Eyelets (large): Reinforcing rings for larger holes.
8. Eyelet punch (large): Used to make a large hole in leather.
9. Eyelet setter (large): Used to set large eyelets.

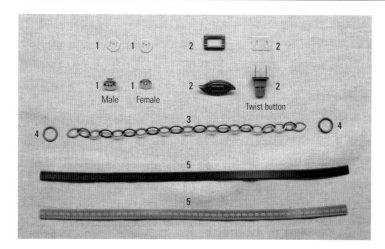

Notions for bags

1. Magnetic snap: Used for purse closure.
2. Twist turn lock: Used for purse closure. Various designs and sizes are available.
3. Chain: Select according to the weight of bag.
4. Jump rings: Used to join chain to purse frame.
5. Leather straps: Used for bag straps and as decoration.

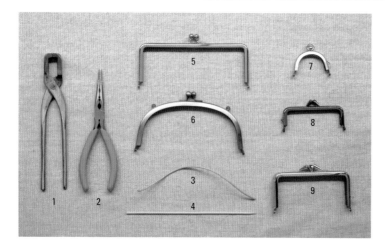

Purse frames and tools

1. Frame crimpers: Used to press the frame from both sides after inserting the fabric. Use a piece of cloth in between to protect the frame from damage.
2. Pliers: Used as a substitute for crimpers.
3. Paper string: To insert into the frame.
4. Bamboo skewer: Use when applying bond into the frame.
5. Purse frame (rounded corners): Used for vanity case (p. 12).
6. Purse frame (with rings): Used for the party purse (p. 28).
7. Purse frame (half-round): Used for small coin purses (p. 10).
8. Purse frame (rounded corners with a ring): Used for seal cases (p. 6).
9. Triple-purse frame (rounded corners): Used for double purse (p. 13).

Basic techniques

How to install rivets

1. Mark the position for a hole on the leather.

2. Make a hole using an eyelet punch by tapping with a mallet.

3. Make a hole in the bag as above.

4. Insert the male rivet into the leather strap hole, and the female rivet into the bag.

5. Insert the shank into the cap.

6. Place the rivet on an anvil, fit the setter on the curve of the rivet head. Tap 4–5 times with a mallet.

7. Completed rivet.

How to install eyelets

1. Make a hole with the punch.

2. Insert the female eyelet as shown and the male from the wrong side of the fabric.

3. Place the eyelet on the anvil as shown, and tap with the setter.

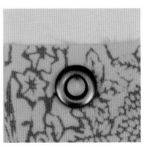

4. Completed eyelet. You can pass a cord or ribbon through it.

How to install a magnetic snap

*A magnetic snap comes as a set with male and female parts and two washers.

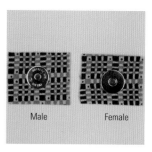

Male   Female

1. Place a washer where you want to install a snap, mark the positions of prongs and cut slits.

2. Put the prongs of the male snap through the slits from the right side of the fabric.

3. On the back side, place the washer over the prongs and bend them open outward.

4. Install the female snap in the same way to complete.

How to install a twist turn lock

*A twist turn lock comes as a set with a twist button/washer and front plate. Reinforce with interfacing as this part is subject to wear.

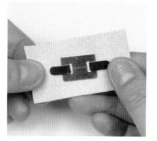

1. Place a washer where you want to install a twist button and cut slits for the prongs.

2. Insert the prongs of the twist button.

3. On the wrong side of the fabric, place the washer over the prongs and bend them open outward to complete installation of the twist button.

4. Cut out a hole by marking its outline using the back part of the front plate.

5. Insert the prongs of the face of the plate into the hole.

6. On the wrong side of the fabric, place the back part of the plate over the prongs and flatten them out to fix.

7. Place the front plate over the twist button.

8. Turn the button to lock.

Instructions

Small coin purse

 p.10

Materials

1. Pattern (p. 84)
2. 2 pcs of exterior fabric (cut out based on the pattern with a 7mm or 0.3in seam allowance)
3. 2 pcs of lining (cut out based on the pattern with a 7mm or 0.3in seam allowance)
4. Purse frame (half-round, 48mm or 1.9in wide)
5. 2 paper strings

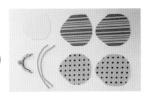

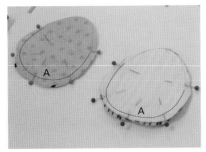

1. Pin right sides of the exterior fabric together while matching the position marks, and sew along the stitch line A. Repeat for the lining.

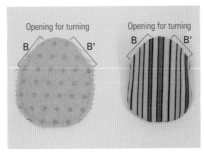

2. Turn the exterior bag right side out.

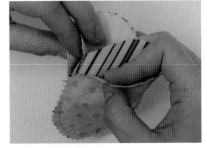

3. Slip the exterior bag in the lining bag, and sew along stitch lines B and B' leaving an opening to turn.

4. Turn the lining right side out. Press the B and B' seams well for a clean finish.

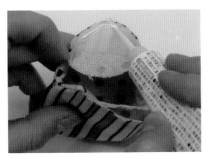

5. Glue the openings with craft bond.

6. Apply purse frame bond using a bamboo skewer.

7. Insert the fabrics into the frame. Make sure to fit them evenly and smoothly.

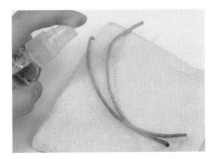

8. Soften the paper strings by wetting.

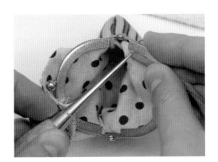

9. Insert the strings using an awl or the like.

10. Flatten the inside of the frame at both ends with the crimpers. Apply force from the outside inward, so that the outer side of the frame will not be damaged.

11. Completed purse.

Double purse

p.13

1. Cut out a medium-weight interfacing based on the pattern and affix to the wrong side of the exterior fabric. Cut out the lining also based on the pattern (no interfacing). Cut out a lightweight interfacing based on the pattern for the divider and affix to the divider fabric.

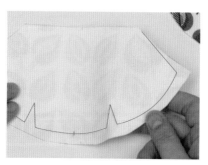

2. Lift the two triangles (above) of the exterior pieces to create volume.

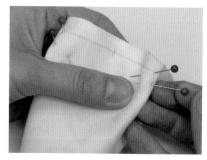

3. Fold each dart triangle in half, pin as above and stitch.

4. The darts help to create the rounded shape.

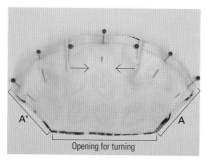

5. Sew the exterior pieces together with the right sides facing, turning the darts on one side as indicated by the arrows above; turn the darts in the opposite direction on the other exterior piece.

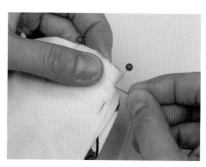

6. Finish both ends with backstitches to reinforce.

7. Finish the cut edges with pinking shears, or cut notches with normal scissors.

8. Press seam allowance open.

9. Turn right side out and smooth the shape.

10. Repeat steps 1 to 9 for the lining. Fold the divider piece in half and apply fusible interfacing with a 7mm or 0.3in seam allowance as shown in step 11.

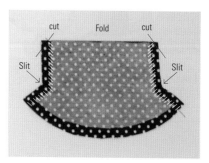

11. Sew together each of the oblique lined areas and trim both top ends diagonally.

12. Before turning right side out, cut slits shown in step 11. for a clean finish.

Materials
1. Patterns (p. 85)
2. 2 pcs of exterior fabric (cut out based on the pattern with a 7mm or 0.3in seam allowance)
3. 2 pcs of lining (cut out based on the pattern with a 7mm or 0.3in seam allowance)
4. 1 pc of fabric for divider
5. Triple-purse frame (rounded corners, 105mm or 4.1in wide)
6. 3 paper strings

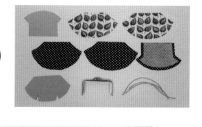

13. The lining fabric comprises three pieces as shown above.

14. Sandwich the divider fabric and sew all three pieces together with the right sides facing.

15. The result will be like this with two compartments.

16. Place the lining over the exterior bag with the right sides facing, and sew stitch lines A and A' of 5.

17. Turn the exterior fabric right side out. Press the seams sewn in step 16.

18. Glue the openings with craft bond.

19. Smooth the bag shape out well before attaching the frame.

20. Apply purse frame bond to the centre frame piece.

21. Insert the divider fabric straight into the frame, and then a string to fix. Fasten both ends of the frame as shown on p. 59.

22. Insert the outer pieces of fabric and strings to the outer frames in the same way to fix.

23. A purse with two compartments results as shown.

24. Completed purse.

Business card case

p. 7

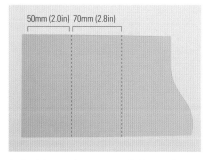

1. Position and score two folds as shown with a tracing spatula on pasteboard.

50mm (2.0in) 70mm (2.8in)

2. Fold using a ruler or the like.

3. Curve the board as shown to produce a neat form.

4. Apply craft bond thinly along the curved part of pasteboard, and attach it to the fabric with a fold allowance (see step 5). If the fabric is thin, do not apply too much bond as it may stain.

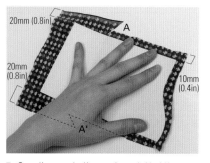

20mm (0.8in)

20mm (0.8in)

10mm (0.4in)

A

A'

5. Cut diagonal slits at A and A'. Allow an extra 20mm (0.8in) for the side folds as above.

A

6. Cut slits in the exterior fabric at A. Apply bond to the pasteboard along the curve, and attach the fabric as shown.

7. Apply bond to the pasteboard along the opposite end section, and while folded, attach to the fabric as above.

8. Apply bond to the remaining sides, and attach them to the fabric.

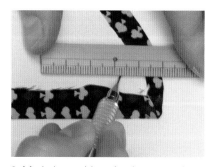

9. Mark the positions for the magnetic snap pieces.

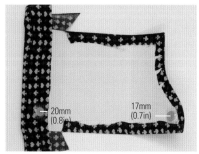

20mm (0.8in)

17mm (0.7in)

10. Ensure the magnetic sides are exposed and glue the snap pieces using craft bond as above.

11. Glue the pocket board onto the wider part of the pocket fabric as above.

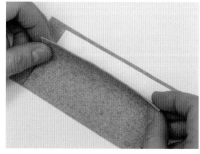

12. Apply bond to the board. Fold the fabric and glue onto the board.

Materials

1. Patterns (pp. 86 to 88)
2. 1 pc of exterior fabric (approx. 130mm x 230mm or 5.1in x 9.1in)
3. 1 pc of pasteboard cut out based on the pattern.
   *Note the grain direction. It is easier to fold in the direction of the grain.
4. 1 pc of the lining cut out based on its pattern.
   *Edge-sealing fabric, e.g. fake suede, is recommended.
5. 1 pc of fabric for pocket partition cut out based on its pattern
6. 1 board for pocket partition (pasteboard or cardboard)
7. 1 set of magnetic snaps (not too thick)

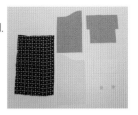

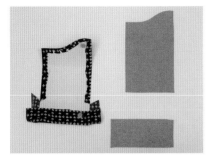

13. The exterior section, lining and pocket partition are ready.

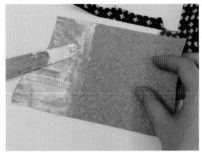

14. Apply bond to the area between the curved end and the first fold.

15. Attach the lining carefully starting along the curve.

16. Apply bond to the other end section as above. Do not glue the middle section.

17. Attach the exterior piece to the above glued section by inserting the pocket partition temporarily to ensure the right thickness.

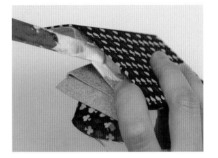

18. Apply the bond as above, while positioning the pocket partition and making the exterior side folds ready.

19. Fold and insert the pocket partition side ends together with the exterior fabric.

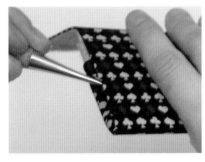

20. Using an awl, push the fabrics inside to avoid bagging.

21. Using the spatula, smooth out any bumps from inside.

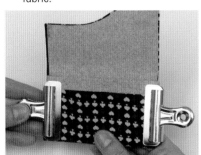

22. Repeat steps 19. to 21. for the other side and secure with clips.

23. To finish the flap, clip while closed with a round stick inserted along the fold to press the bonding and form a curve.

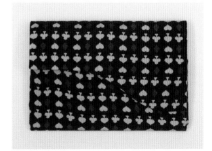

24. Completed case.

TRIED IT ?

Things to note

Most of the stitching shown in this book was done by machine. If you want to sew any of the small items by hand, I recommend making your stitches as fine as possible for a clean finish.

Fusible interfacing

I have used multiple types of fusible interfacings according to the fabric and application, including a lightweight non-woven interfacing for pocket linings, a medium-weight for purses and bags, a heavy-weight interfacing when a stiff and strong finish was needed, or an adhesive-type interfacing for a strong base or gusset. However, there are no rules, nor always a necessity to use interfacings, particularly if you use thick and strong fabric such as an obi as the main material.

It is easy to apply interfacings to cotton fabrics, but take extra care when using a thin silk material such as kimono fabric. Start with a lightweight interfacing and layer with another if necessary to prevent creases or migration of the interfacing's glue to the fabric surface.

Seam/fold allowance

Cut materials based on their patterns or given dimensions with a 7mm (0.3in) seam allowance. I allow 15mm to 20mm (0.6in to 0.8in) for the fold in parts of purses and bags. Press the seam allowance open for a neat finish and to prevent it becoming too bulky.

Cutting edge

All items in this book are lined and the raw cut edges were finished with pinking shears. If you do not have pinking shears, finish with zigzag stitches. Finish with pinking shears or cut notches on curved edges for a smooth curve when the fabric is turned right side out.

Seal case
p. 6

Materials
1. Patterns (p. 84)
2. 1 pc of exterior fabric (68mm x 102mm or 2.7in x 4.0in)
3. 1 pc adhesive interfacing (68mm x 82mm or 2.7in x 3.2in)
4. 1 pc of lining (fake suede/68mm x 80mm or 2.7in x 3.1in)
5. Purse frame (rounded corners, 85mm or 3.3in wide)

---

1. Cut out the interfacing based on its pattern.
2. Attach interfacing to the exterior fabric. Cut out the exterior fabric with fold allowances (10mm x 20mm or 0.4in x 08in) at the centre of each side. Fold and attach them to the inside with craft bond.
3. Cut out the lining based on the pattern.
4. Place the lining on the exterior fabric. Apply bond to the centre of each side only (over the fold allowances), fold in half as shown and join the glued parts together.
5. Insert the fabrics into the purse frame (see steps 5 to 10, p. 59) to finish.

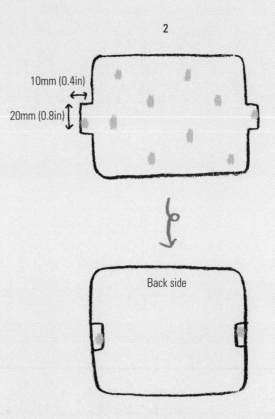

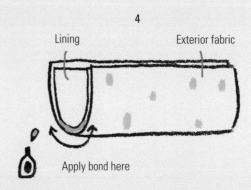

Coasters
p. 8

Materials

1. Patterns (p. 89)
2. 1 pc of exterior fabric (150mm x 120mm or 5.9in x 4.7in)
3. 1 pc of fusible interfacing
   (medium weight/150mm x 120mm or 5.9in x 4.7in)
4. 1 pc of lining (150mm x 120mm or 5.9in x 4.7in)
5. Buttons or charms (optional)

1. Attach the interfacing onto the pattern of the exterior fabric and cut out with a 7mm (0.3in) seam allowance.
2. Cut out the lining based on the pattern with a 7mm (0.3in) seam allowance. *The pattern in step 1 can be used in reverse.
3. Attach button(s) or charm(s), if using any, at this stage.
4. Stitch the exterior fabric and lining together with the right sides facing, leaving an opening for turning.
5. Clip the seam allowances with small intervals and turn right side out.
6. Press and hand-stitch the opening closed to finish.

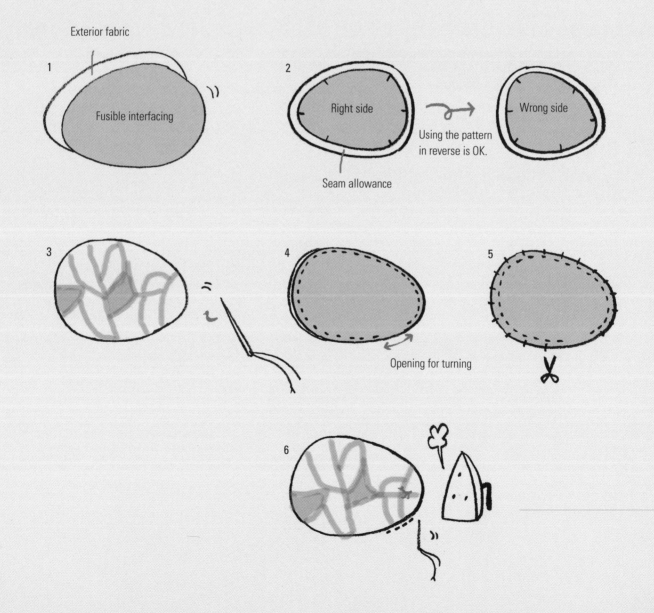

Exterior fabric

1 Fusible interfacing

2 Right side — Seam allowance — Wrong side
Using the pattern in reverse is OK.

3

4 Opening for turning

5

6

66

Covered buttons
p. 9

Materials

1. Exterior fabric sufficient to cover a button
2. A button covering kit
3. 1 pc of fusible interfacing (lightweight/optional)

1. Cut out the fabric based on the pattern provided in the kit.
   *For sheer fabrics, line with interfacing cut to the same size.
2. Cover the button shell with fabric and set it in the mould.
3. Press the button back down onto the button shell.
4. Press down on the button back with the pusher to finish.

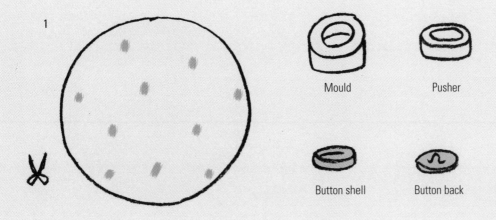

1

Mould

Pusher

Button shell

Button back

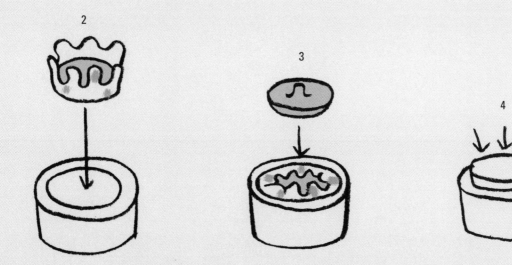

2

3

4

Vanity case
p. 12

Materials

1. Pattern (p. 90)

2. 2 pcs of exterior fabric (185mm x 224mm or 7.3in x 8.8in)

3. 2 pcs of fusible interfacing
   (medium weight/185 x 224mm or 7.3in x 8.8in)

4. 2 pcs of lining (185mm x 224mm or 7.3in x 8.8in)

5. Purse frame (rounded corners, 150mm or 5.9in wide)

1. Cut out two pieces each of the exterior fabric lined with interfacing and the lining without interfacing, with a 7mm (0.3in) seam allowance, except for the top edge. Trim the seam allowance diagonally at B as shown below.

2. Join two pieces each of the exterior fabric and lining together with right sides facing, by sewing along stitch line A.

3. Press seam allowances of the exterior and lining fabrics open at B and B' (see steps 7–8, p. 60), to make approx. 30mm (1.2in) gussets. Cut 10mm (0.4in) off the end.

4. Turn the right side of the exterior bag out, slip it in the lining bag and join them by stitching B and B' (see steps 2–4, p. 59). Turn the right side out and smooth the shape.

5. Insert the fabrics into the purse frame (see steps 5–10, p. 59) to finish.

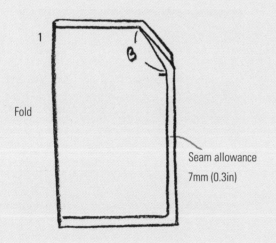

Fold

Seam allowance
7mm (0.3in)

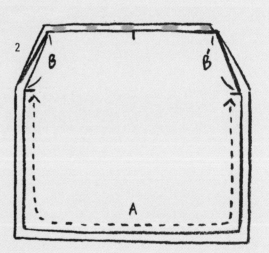

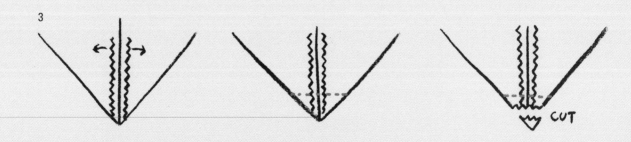

Notebook cover
p. 14

Materials

1. 1 notebook (120mm x 85mm or 4.7in x 3.3in)
   *Rhodia No. 12 is used here.

2. 1 pc of exterior fabric (113mm x 390mm or 4.4in x 15.4in)

3. 1 pc of fusible interfacing
   (medium weight/93mm x 370mm or 3.7in x 14.6in)

4. 1 pc of lining
   (fake suede/90mm x 367mm or 3.5in x 14.4in)

5. Ribbon or cord for pen holder (50mm or 2.0in long)

---

1. Attach interfacing to the exterior fabric with a 10mm (0.4in) margin for bond. Note the direction of the fabric pattern of the front cover section.

2. Apply craft bond to the margin of the interfacing and fold inward to affix.

3. Attach the lining to the inside of the exterior fabric. When attaching a pen holder, fold a ribbon in half and insert under the lining as shown before finally gluing down.

4. Sew the left edge of section A and the right edge of B.

5. Fold sections A and B inward and sew the top and bottom edges of the flaps as shown. *Score the fold lines of section A and B with a tracing spatula for easy folding.

6. Insert a notebook to finish. The design can be applied to any size of notebook when the rules for the allowances as shown are followed.

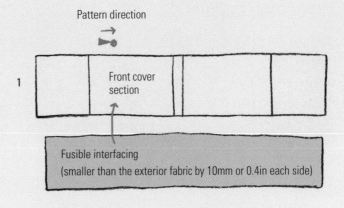

Pattern direction

1 — Front cover section

Fusible interfacing
(smaller than the exterior fabric by 10mm or 0.4in each side)

2

Ribbon or cord
15mm (0.6in)

15mm (0.6in)

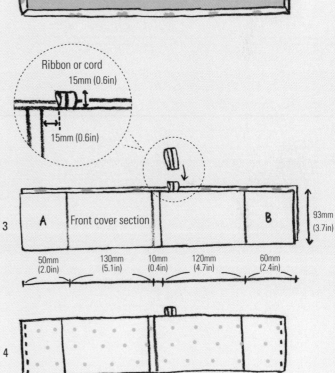

3

A | Front cover section | B

93mm (3.7in)

50mm (2.0in) | 130mm (5.1in) | 10mm (0.4in) | 120mm (4.7in) | 60mm (2.4in)

4

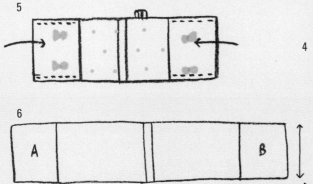

5

6

A | B

Size of notebook
+
8mm (0.3in)

Size of notebook
+
10mm (0.4in)

Thickness of notebook

Size of notebook

If you follow these rules, any size of notebook can be used.

Pencil/pen case

p. 15

Materials

1. Pattern (p. 91)
2. 1 pc of exterior fabric (180mm x 254mm or 7.1in x 10.0in)
3. 1 pc of fusible interfacing
   (medium weight/180 x 254mm or 7.1in x 10.0in)
4. 1 pc of lining (180mm x 254mm or 7.1in x 10.0in)
5. Zipper (200mm or 7.8in long)

1. Cut out the exterior fabric and the lining based on the pattern with a 7mm (0.3in) seam allowance, except for sides A and A' which should be 15mm (0.6in). Line the exterior fabric with interfacing.
2. Fold the allowances at A and A' towards the inside.
3. Stitch one side of the zipper to A as shown.
4. Stitch the other side of zipper to A' (this is a little difficult as it involves a tubular form). Keep the zipper open.
5. Join B and B' with the right sides facing.
6. Press the seam allowance at B and B' open and stitch C and C' to it. Stitch D and D' to E in the same way.
7. In the same way stich F and F' to G, and then join H and H' to G.
8. Sew the lining in the same way as the exterior case, following steps 2 to 7.
9. Insert the lining case in the exterior case with the wrong sides facing and attach them by hemstitching.
10. Hand stitch at the bottom to prevent the case lining from moving.

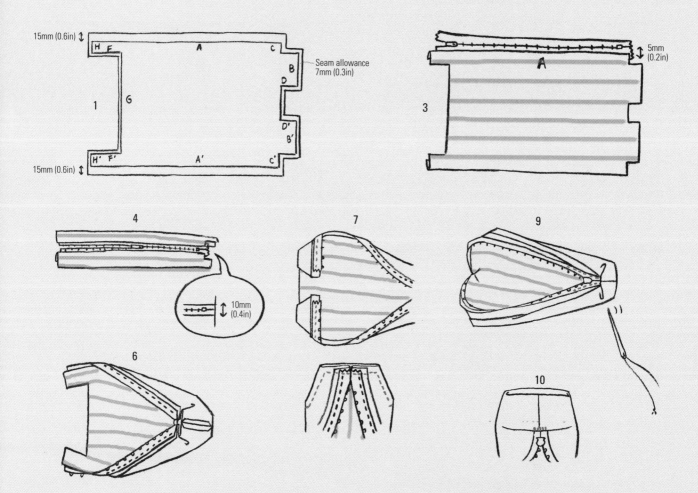

Lampshade
p. 16

Materials

1. Fabric (amount based on the lampshade frame ring size)
2. Pendant socket (desired length)
3. 1 C-ring (130mm or 5.1in diameter used here)
4. 1 bottom frame ring with the same diameter as the top one
5. Glass fibre sheet (or other heat resistant material e.g. PP sheet)
6. Other decorative parts (optional)

1. Roll a sheet of glass fibre, the base of the shade, around the C-ring to measure the required length. Cut out the sheet to the size of the 'measured length + 15mm (0.6in) x the desired height', and mark the position at 15mm (0.6in) from the edge.
2. Cut out the fabric larger than the glass fibre sheet by 10mm (0.4in) on all sides.
3. Attach the fabric to the glass fibre sheet.
4. Fold the margin in at both ends and affix with craft bond.
5. Roll the shade and glue the ends by overlapping the 15mm (0.6in) margin to make a tube.
6. Insert the C-ring at the top of the shade. Apply craft bond to the ring and attach the fabric by wrapping it around the ring.
7. Insert another ring with the same size at the bottom and glue in the same way as in step 6.
8. Install a pendant socket to finish. You can decorate the bottom edge with pieces of crystal glass or beads for a glittering effect when lit.

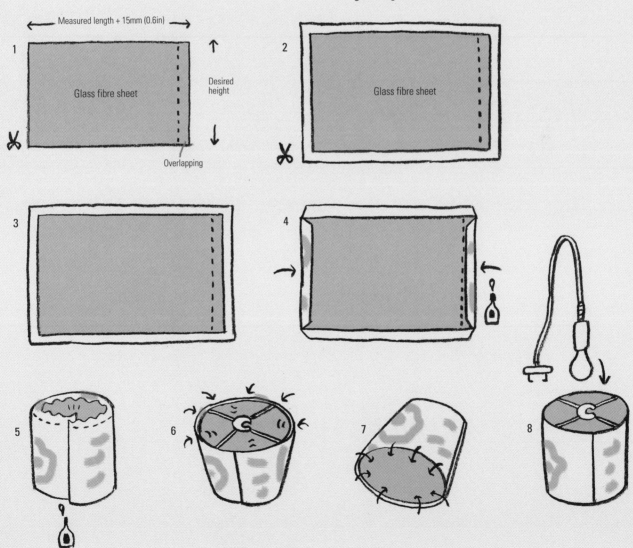

Multi-bags

p. 18

Finished dimensions
Main bag: 200mm (W) x 230mm (H) or 7.9in (W) x 9.1in (H)
Handle: 120cm or 47.2in (pochette)/280mm or 11.0in (tote bag) long

Materials

1. 1 pc of exterior fabric (214mm x 490mm or 8.4in x 19.3in)

2. 1 pc of fusible interfacing
   (medium weight/200mm x 460mm or 7.9in x 18.1in)

3. 1 pc of lining (214mm x 490mm or 8.4in x 19.3in)

4. 1 pc of inner pocket fabric
   (124mm x 194mm or 4.9in x 7.6in)

5. 1 pc of inner pocket fusible interfacing
   (lightweight/110mm x 90mm or 4.3in x 3.5in)

6. 4 sets of eyelets (inner diameter: 6mm or 0.2in)

7. Leather cord or ribbon: 138cm or 54.3in (leather cord,
   p. 18)/100cm or 39.4in (ribbon, p. 19)

1. Apply fusible interfacing to the exterior fabric with seam allowance as shown below.

2. Stitch both sides of the fabric to make a bag.

3. Cut out the lining and stitch as above to make a bag.

4. Fold the pocket fabric in half and attach the interfacing as shown below. *Trim the corners diagonally as shown for a neat finish.

5. Stitch around the edge except the opening for turning, and turn the right side out. Sew the pocket onto the lining as shown. Add triangular stitches at the top corners to reinforce the pocket.

6. Sew the exterior and lining fabrics together with the right sides facing. Turn the right side out.

7. Install eyelets at the top of the bag as shown below.

8. Insert a leather cord or ribbon through the eyelets to finish. *Adjust the handle length at the knots.

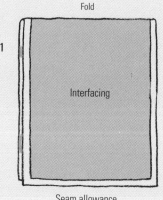

1 — Fold / Interfacing / Seam allowance

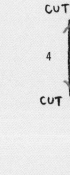

4 — CUT / Fold / CUT / Interfacing / CUT / CUT / Opening for turning

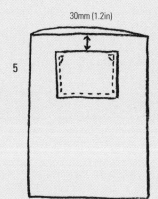

5 — 30mm (1.2in)

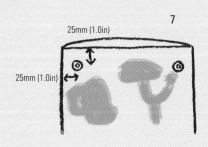

7 — 25mm (1.0in) / 25mm (1.0in)

8

Double-sided bag

p. 20

Finished dimensions

Main bag: 260mm (W) x 350mm (H) x 40mm (D) or 10.2in (W) x 13.8 (H) x 1.6in (D)

Handle: 380mm or 15.0in long

Materials

1. 1 pc of cotton-linen interfacing
   (medium weight/754mm x 274mm or 29.7in x 10.8in)

2. 1 pc of exterior fabric
   (384mm x 274mm or 15.1in x 10.8in)

3. 1 pc of lining fabric (754mm x 274mm or 29.7in x 10.8in)

4. 1 pc of inner pocket fabric
   (154mm x 154mm or 6.1in x 6.1in)

5. 1 pc of fusible interfacing for inner pocket
   (lightweight/140mm x 140mm or 5.5in x 5.5in)

6. Strap for handle
   (braided waxed strap: 440mm or 17.3in long)

7. Gold metallic machine-sewing thread

1. Sew the exterior fabric onto the cotton-linen interfacing by stitching on the right side. *Use gold metallic thread wound onto a bobbin for the lower thread.

2. Fold 1. in half and sew both sides to make a bag.

3. Press the seams of 2. open and make gussets (40mm or 1.6in wide).

4. Fold the pocket fabric in half and attach the interfacing as shown below. *Trim the corners diagonally as shown for a neat finish.

5. Sew the pocket (4.) onto the lining as shown (see step 5 on p. 72).

6. Slip the exterior bag into the lining bag with the right sides facing, insert the handles between them and sew together except the opening for turning.

7. Turn right side out. Add two rows of topstitching, at 2mm (0.1in) and 12mm to 18mm (0.5in to 0.7in) from the top edge.

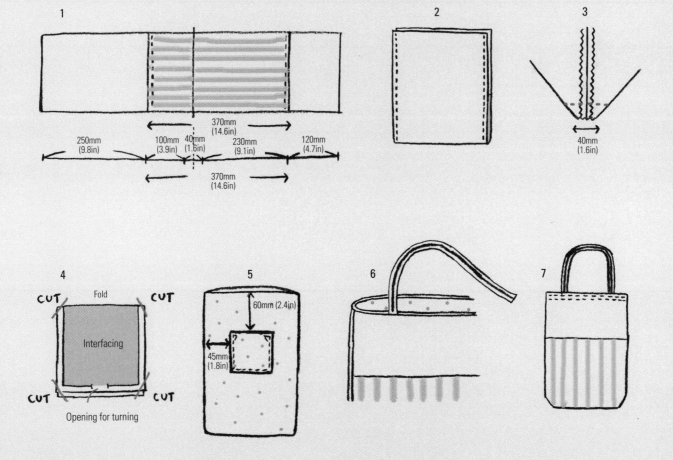

Square bag

p. 22

Finished dimensions
Main bag: 270mm (W) x 240mm (H) x 130mm (D) or 10.6in (W) x 9.4in (H) x 5.1in (D)
Handle: 300mm or 11.8in long

Materials

1. 2 pcs of exterior front fabric
   (257mm x 284mm or 10.1in x 11.2in)

2. 2 pcs of fusible interfacing
   (heavy weight/270mm x 240mm or 10.6in x 9.4in)

3. 1 pc of adhesive interfacing
   (130mm x 750mm or 5.1in x 29.5in) *Use 2 pcs if
   necessary.

4. 2 pcs of denim side fabric
   (392mm x 144mm or 15.4in x 5.7in)

5. 1 set of lining fabric (same size as the exterior front
   fabric and denim side fabric.)

6. 1 pc of inner pocket fabric
   (154mm x 294mm or 6.1in x 11.6in)

7. 1 pc of inner pocket fusible interfacing
   (lightweight/140mm x 140mm or 5.5in x 5.5in)

8. 2 tapes for handle (45mm x 440mm or 1.8in x 17.3in)

1. Stitch the two pieces of denim to make a long gusset.
   Press the seam open and topstitch from the right side as
   shown.

2. Sew the gusset and two pieces of the exterior fabric
   together to make a bag.

3. Fold the pocket fabric in half and attach the interfacing as
   shown below. *Trim the corners diagonally as shown for a
   neat finish.

4. Sew the pocket onto the lining at 60mm (2.4in) from the
   top edge (see step 5, p. 72), and sew the lining pieces
   together to make a bag.

5. Layer the tapes and stitch along one long edge to make a
   wider piece for the handle.

6. Place the exterior and lining bags together with right sides
   facing. Inserting one end of the tape between them, stitch
   along the top edge, leaving an opening for turning, where
   the other end of the tape will be inserted later.

7. Turn the right side of the bag out, insert the other end of
   the tape into the opening and stitch to close.

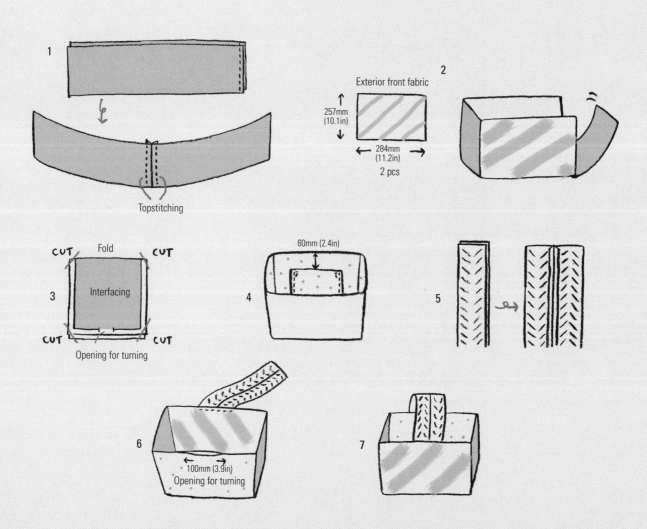

Tote bag using obi fabric

p. 24

Finished dimensions
Main bag: 230mm (W) x 310mm (H) x 80mm (D) or 9.1in (W) x 12.2in (H) x 3.1in (D)
Handle: 455mm or 17.9in long

Materials

1. 2 pcs each of the exterior fabric (obi/244mm x 332mm or 9.6in x 13.0in + 44mm x 94mm or 1.7in x 3.7in)

2. 2 pcs of adhesive interfacing (430mm x 80mm or 17.0in x 3.1in)

3. 2 pcs each of the lining (234mm x 332mm or 9.2in x 13.0in + 425mm x 80mm or 16.7in x 3.1in)

4. 1 pc of inner pocket fabric (154mm x 294mm or 6.1in x 11.6in)

5. 1 pc of inner pocket fusible interfacing (140mm x 140mm or 5.5in x 5.5in)

6. 2 leather straps (90mm or 3.5in wide): 535mm or 21.1in long

7. 4 sets of eyelets (inner diameter: 13mm or 0.5in)

8. 4 sets of rivets

1. Stitch the two long exterior gusset pieces together.

2. Press the seam open and topstitch from the right side as shown.

3. Sew 2. and two pieces of the exterior fabric (front and back) together to make a bag.

4. Fold the pocket fabric in half and attach the interfacing as shown below. *Trim the corners diagonally as shown for a neat finish.

5. Sew the pocket onto the lining as shown below (see step 5, p. 72)

6. Sew the lining pieces together to make a bag as in steps 1 to 3 above, leaving a 150mm (5.9in) opening for turning.

7. Place the exterior and lining bags together with right sides facing, and stitch together along the top edge.

8. Turn the right side out through the opening, and shape the bag.

9. Install eyelets at four positions as shown below (see p. 57).

10. Insert the leather straps through the eyelets, fold 40mm (1.6in) back and fasten with rivets (see p. 57).

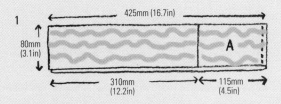

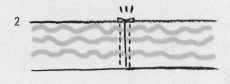

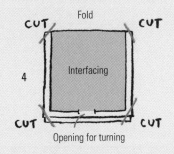

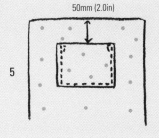

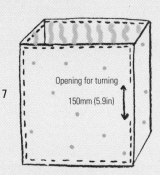

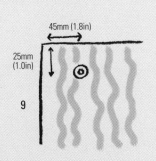

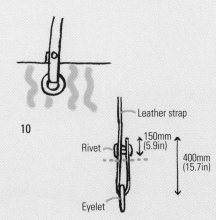

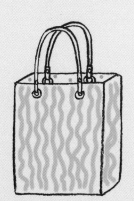

Little bird bag

p. 26

Finished dimensions
Main bag: 170mm (W) x 200mm (H) x 30mm (D) or 6.7in (W) x 7.9in (H) x 1.2in (D)
Handle: 270mm or 10.6in (tote bag)/380mm or 15.0in (shoulder bag)/121cm or 4.8in (pochette)

Materials

1. Pattern (p. 92)

2. 2 pcs of exterior fabric
   (242mm x 368mm or 9.5in x 14.5in)

3. 2 pcs of fusible interfacing
   (medium weight/242mm x 368mm or 9.5in x 14.5in)

4. 2 pcs of lining (242mm x 368mm or 9.5in x 14.5in)

5. 1 pc of inner pocket fabric
   (124mm x 194mm or 4.9in x 7.6in)

6. 1 pc of inner pocket fusible interfacing
   (lightweight/110mm x 90mm or 4.3in x 3.5in)

7. Leather strap (90mm or 3.5in wide):
   340mm or 13.4in (tote bag)
   460mm or 18.1in (shoulder bag)
   129cm or 50.8in (pochette)

8. Buttons or charms (optional)

9. 4 sets of rivets

1. Cut out the exterior and lining fabrics based on the pattern with a 7mm (0.3in) seam allowance, except for the top (15mm or 0.6in). Attach fusible interfacing to the exterior fabric.

2. Fold the pocket fabric in half and apply the interfacing as shown below. *Trim the corners diagonally as shown for a neat finish.

3. Stitch around the edge of the pocket except the opening for turning, and turn right side out.

4. Sew the pocket onto the lining B at 50mm (2.0in) from the top edge (see step 5, p. 72). *Attach button(s) or charm(s), if using any, at this stage.

5. Sew together the exterior and lining fabrics with the right sides facing.

6. Press the seam allowances open, making an approx. 30mm (1.2in) gusset (*at the curved side only). Trim 10mm (0.4in) off the end.

7. Place the exterior and lining bags together with the right sides facing, and stitch together along the top edge leaving an opening for turning.

8. Turn right side out through the opening, and shape the bag. Topstitch at 3mm (0.1in) from the top edge to finish the main part. Secure the gusset by hand stitching.

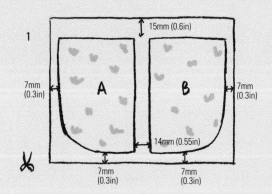

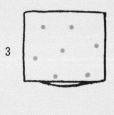

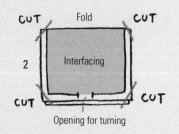

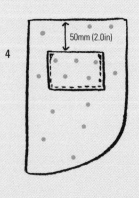

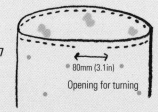

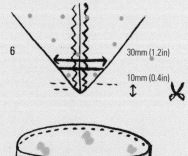

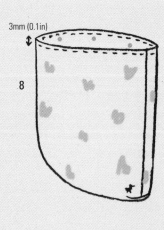

[Tote bag type] *see 'How to install rivets' on p. 57

1. Make two holes in the leather strap.

2. Mark position and make holes in the bag.

3. Install rivets at two places each on the front and back.

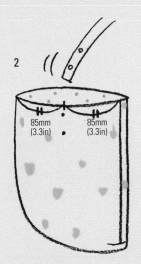

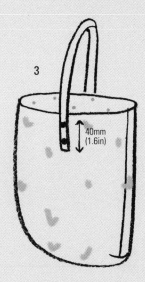

[Shoulder bag and pochette type] *see 'How to install rivets' on p. 57

1. Make two holes in the leather strap.

2. Make holes in the bag away from the seams to avoid stress on the seams.

3. Install rivets at two points each on the front and back.

Party purse with chain
p. 28

Materials

1. Pattern (p. 93)

2. 2 pcs of exterior fabric
   (obi/202mm x 214mm or 8.0in x 8.4in)

3. 2 pcs of fusible interfacing (medium weight/195mm
   x 200mm or 7.7in x 7.9in (*Use the same size as the
   exterior fabric when it is light in weight.)

4. 2 pcs of lining (202mm x 214mm or 8.0in x 8.4in)

5. 1 pc of inner pocket fabric (124mm x 194mm or 4.9in x
   7.6in)

6. 1 pc of inner pocket fusible interfacing
   (lightweight/110mm x 90mm 4.3in x 3.5in)

7. Decorative items (optional)

8. Chain (340mm or 13.4in long)

9. Purse frame with rings (145mm or 5.7in wide)

10. 2 jump rings (13mm or 0.5in) *Ensure rings are durable.

1. Cut out the exterior and lining fabrics based on the pattern
   with a 7mm (0.3in) seam allowance. Attach fusible
   interfacing to the exterior fabric.

2. Join the exterior pieces with the right sides facing, by
   stitching between the marks (A) below.

3. Fold the pocket fabric in half and attach the interfacing as
   shown below. *Trim the corners diagonally as shown for a
   neat finish.

4. Sew the pocket onto the lining at 50mm (2.0in) from
   the top edge (see step 5, p. 72). Sew the lining pieces
   together to make a bag as in step 2 above.

5. Join the exterior and lining bags together with the right
   sides facing, by stitching along the edge, leaving an
   opening for turning.

6. Turn right side out and shape the bag. Insert the fabrics
   into the purse frame (see steps 5–10 on p. 59).

7. Attach the chain to the frame using the jump rings to
   finish.

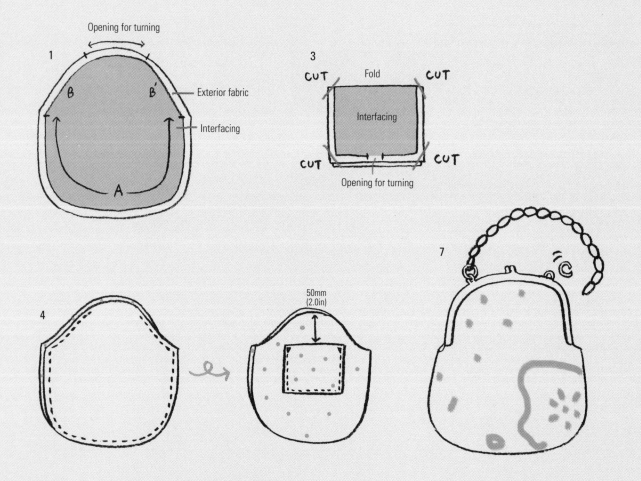

Clutch purse

p. 28

Finished dimensions
240mm (W) x 140mm (H) or 9.4in (W) x 5.5in (H)

Materials

1. 1 pc of exterior fabric
   (obi/254mm x 412mm or 10.0in x 16.2in)

2. 1 pc of adhesive interfacing
   (240mm x 360mm or 9.4in x 14.2in)

3. 1 pc of lining (254mm x 367mm or 10.0in x 14.4in)

4. 1 pc of inner pocket fabric
   (124mm x 194mm or 4.9in x 7.6in)

5. 1 pc of inner pocket fusible interfacing
   (lightweight/110mm x 90mm or 4.3in x 3.5in)

6. 1 set of magnetic snaps

7. 1 pc of adhesive interfacing for the magnetic snap
   reinforcement (30mm x 40mm or 1.2in x 1.6in)

1. Cut out the exterior fabric and lining as below.

2. Fold the pocket fabric in half and attach the interfacing as
   shown below, and sew it onto the lining at 30mm (1.2in)
   from the edge (see step 5, p. 72).

3. Fold section A towards B of the exterior fabric with the
   right sides facing inside, and sew both side edges to make
   a bag. Repeat for the lining.

4. Install the male snap on the right side of section D (see p.
   58). Affix interfacing to the reverse side.

5. Affix the adhesive interfacing to the wrong side of the
   exterior fabric, and install the female snap on the right
   side of section A.

6. Join the exterior piece and lining bag together with the
   right sides facing, by stitching along the edge except for
   the opening D. *Note that the area where A and B are
   layered is difficult to sew.

7. Turn right side out and hemstitch the turned edge to finish.

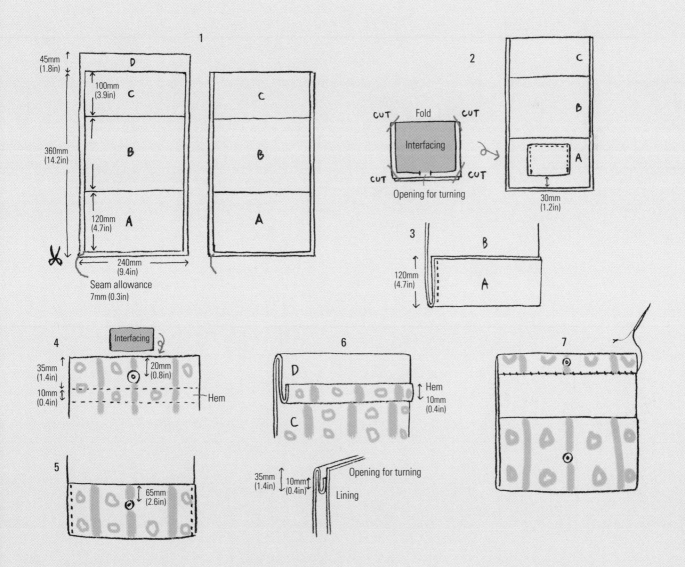

Leather/fabric combination bag

p. 30

Finished dimensions
Main bag: 250mm (W) x 390mm (max. H)/260mm (min. H) x 25mm (D) or
9.8in (W) x 15.4in (max. H)/10.2in (min. H) x 1.0in (D)
Handle: 460mm or 18.1in long

Materials

1. 2 pcs of calfskin (or other leather soft enough for sewing machine/194mm x 564mm or 7.6in x 22.2in)

2. 2 pcs of exterior fabric (obi/194mm x 564mm or 7.6in x 22.2in)

3. 4 pcs of lining (194mm x 564mm or 7.6in x 22.2in)

4. 2 pcs of fusible interfacing (medium weight/180mm x 550mm or 7.1in x 21.7in)

5. 2 pcs of inner pocket fabric (157mm x 294mm + 234mm x 374mm or 6.2in x 11.6in + 9.2in x 14.7in)

6. 2 pcs of inner pocket fusible interfacing (lightweight/140mm x 140mm + 220mm x 180mm or 5.5in x 5.5in + 8.7in x 7.1in)

7. 2 strips of calfskin for piping (enough for pocket width)

8. Strap for handle (braided waxed strap: 320mm x 500mm or 12.6in x 19.7in)

9. 1 set of magnetic snaps

10. 2 pcs of adhesive interfacing (250mm x 500mm or 9.8in x 19.7in)

1. Cut out the calfskin and exterior fabric as shown below. Apply fusible interfacing to the exterior fabric.

2. Sew the pieces together to form a windmill shape as shown below, to make the bag bottom.

3. Sew A and A', B and B', C and C', and D and D' respectively.

4. Sew the lining in the same way as above.

5. Fold the pocket fabric in half and attach the interfacing as shown below. Place calfskin piping along the top edge of both pockets.

6. Sew the pocket onto the lining as shown below (see step 5, p. 72)

7. Affix adhesive interfacing above the pocket, and install magnetic snap as below (see p. 58).

8. Sew the exterior and lining bags together with right sides facing, except for the opening for turning where the handle will be inserted later. Turn the right side out. Hand stitch at the bottom four corners to prevent the bag lining from moving.

9. Fold the unfinished top calfskin ends to form triangles, insert the handle and attach with multiple topstitches in a triangular pattern. Stitch along the top edge at 3mm (0.1in) down to finish.

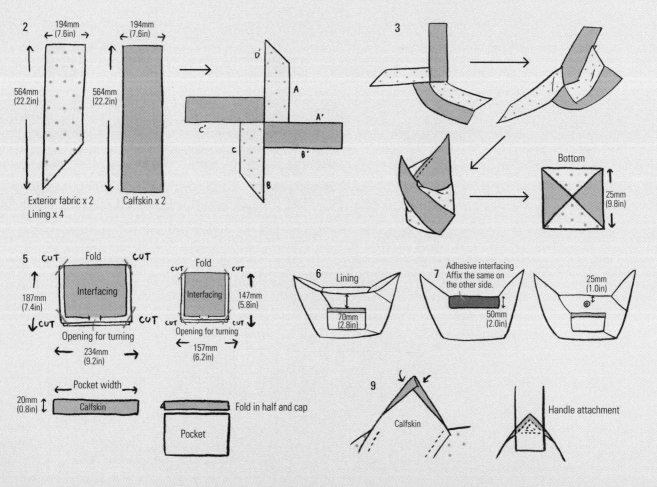

City bag

p. 43

Finished dimensions
Main bag: 260mm (W) x 215mm (H) x 40mm (D) or 10.2in (W) x 8.5in (H) x 1.6in (D)
Handle: 305mm or 12.0in long
*The following instructions are for the bag using two different exterior fabrics.

Materials

1. Pattern (p. 94)

2. 2 pcs of base exterior fabric (cotton-linen, medium weight/227mm x 304mm or 8.9in x 12.0in) *Affix the same size interfacing when using thin fabric.

3. 1 pc of exterior fabric for bottom section (280mm x 85mm or 11.0in x 3.3in)

4. 2 pcs of lining (227mm x 304mm or 8.9in x 12.0in)

5. 1 pc of inner pocket fabric (124mm x 194mm or 4.9in x 7.6in)

6. 1 pc of inner pocket fusible interfacing (lightweight/110mm x 90mm or 4.3in x 3.5in)

7. 2 leather straps (410mm or 16.1in long)

8. 8 sets of rivets

9. Purse frame (without rings/190mm or 7.5in wide)

---

1. Cut out the base exterior and lining fabrics based on the pattern with a 7mm (0.3in) seam allowance.

2. Sew the exterior fabric (bottom section) onto the base exterior fabric.

3. Join the exterior pieces by sewing along the stitch line A below, press the seam allowances open, and topstitch from the right side. *Sew on any decorative parts at this stage.

4. Sew the stitch lines B and B', press seam allowances open and make gussets. The frame hinges will sit at the top ends.

5. Fold the pocket fabric in half and attach the interfacing as shown below. *Trim the corners diagonally as shown for a neat finish.

6. Sew the pocket onto the lining at 70mm (2.8in) from the top edge (see step 5, p. 72). Sew the lining pieces together in the same way as the exterior pieces to make a bag. Press the seam allowances open.

7. Place the exterior and lining bags together with the right sides facing, by joining at the flap ends and sewing along the stitch lines C and C', leaving an opening for turning. Turn right side out.

8. Insert the fabrics into the purse frame (see steps 5–10, p. 59).

9. Attach the leather strap as shown below with rivets (see p. 57).

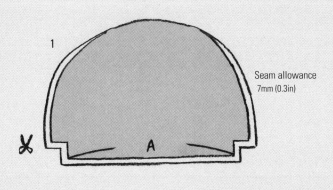

Seam allowance
7mm (0.3in)

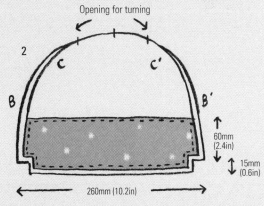

Opening for turning

60mm (2.4in)

15mm (0.6in)

260mm (10.2in)

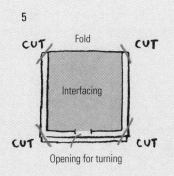

Fold

CUT CUT

Interfacing

CUT CUT

Opening for turning

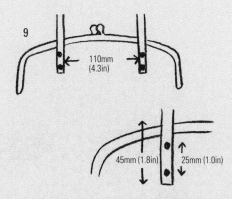

110mm (4.3in)

45mm (1.8in)   25mm (1.0in)

Cube bag

p. 43

Finished dimensions
Main bag: 160mm (W) x 160mm (H) x 116mm (D) or 6.3in (W) x 6.3in (H) x 4.6in (D)
Handle: 390mm or 15.4in long

Materials

1. 1 pc of exterior fabric (size: as in drawing 2)

2. 1 pc of fusible interfacing (heavy weight/size: exterior fabric minus seam allowances)

3. 1 pc of lining (size: as in drawing 2)

4. 1 pc of adhesive interfacing

5. 1 pc of inner pocket fabric
(124mm x 194mm or 4.9in x 7.6in)

6. 1 pc of inner pocket fusible interfacing
(lightweight/110mm x 90mm or 4.3in x 3.5in)

7. 2 cords or ribbons for the inner lids (180mm or 7.1in long)

8. 1 twist turn lock

9. 2 leather straps (9mm x 410mm or 0.4in x 16.1in)

10. 8 sets of rivets

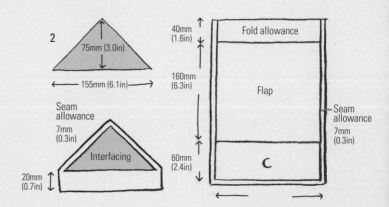

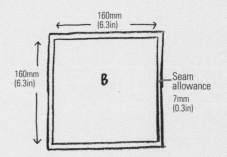

1. Cut out the interfacing for two inner lids, A and B as shown in drawing 2.

2. Affix the interfacing to the exterior fabric, and cut out with a 7mm (0.3in) seam allowance. *Allow 20mm (0.8in) for the bottom of the inner lid only.

3. Cut out the lining in the same way as the exterior pieces.

4. Make the inner lids. Place the exterior and lining pieces with right sides facing, insert the cord or ribbon ends in between and stitch together. Turn right side out and topstitch.

5. Fold the pocket fabric in half and attach the interfacing (see step 5, p. 81).

6. Sew the pocket onto lining A at 40mm (1.6in) from the top edge (see step 5, p. 72).

7. Join A and B of the exterior fabric to make a cube shape. Repeat for the lining. Affix adhesive interfacing to the bottom of the exterior cube.

8. Turn out the right sides of both the exterior and lining cubes. Insert the inner lids and the flap in between, and stitch together.

9. Mark a fold on the flap at 60mm (2.4in) from the edge with a tracing spatula.

10. Install the plate of a twist turn lock on section C, and the twist button as shown in drawing 10 (see p. 58).

11. Attach the leather strap on the sides with rivets as shown.

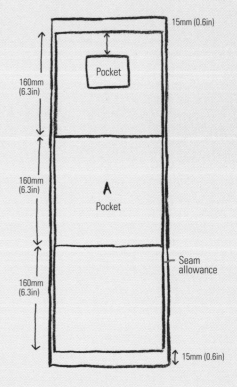

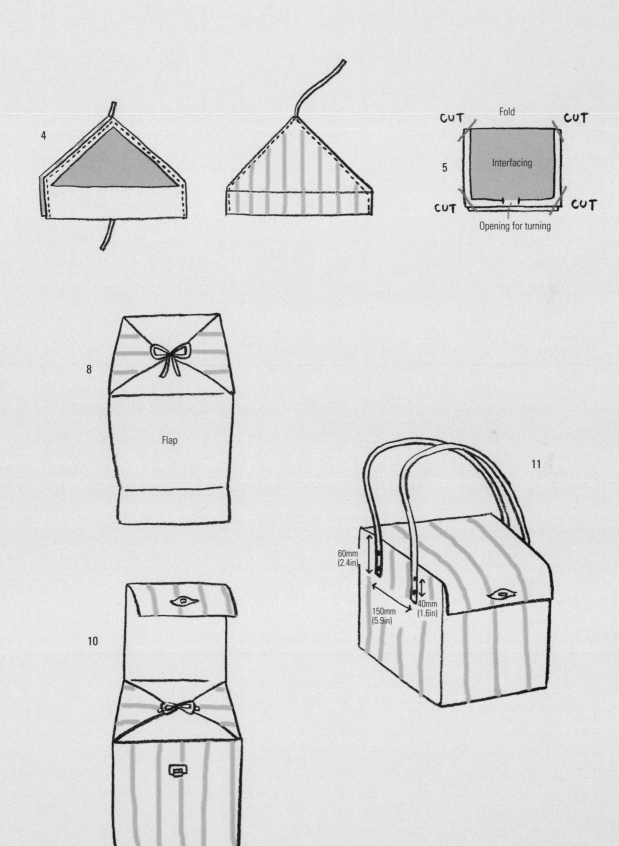

4

5 Fold
CUT   CUT
Interfacing
CUT   CUT
Opening for turning

8 Flap

10

11
60mm
(2.4in)
150mm
(5.9in)
40mm
(1.6in)

Patterns

Small coin purse
(Instructions on p. 59)

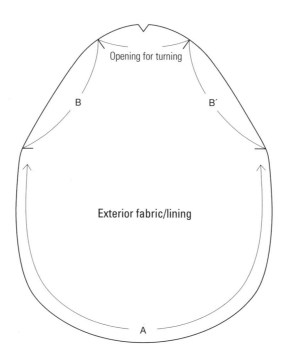

Opening for turning

B   B´

Exterior fabric/lining

A

Seal case
(Instructions on p. 65)

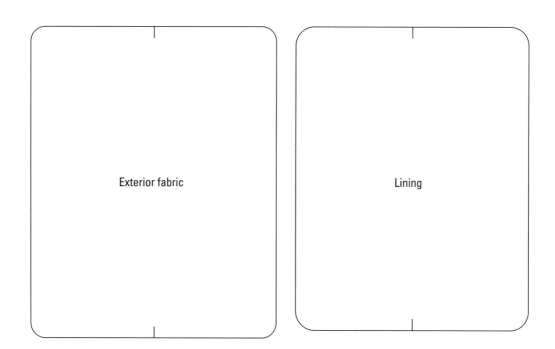

Exterior fabric

Lining

Double purse
(Instructions on p. 60)

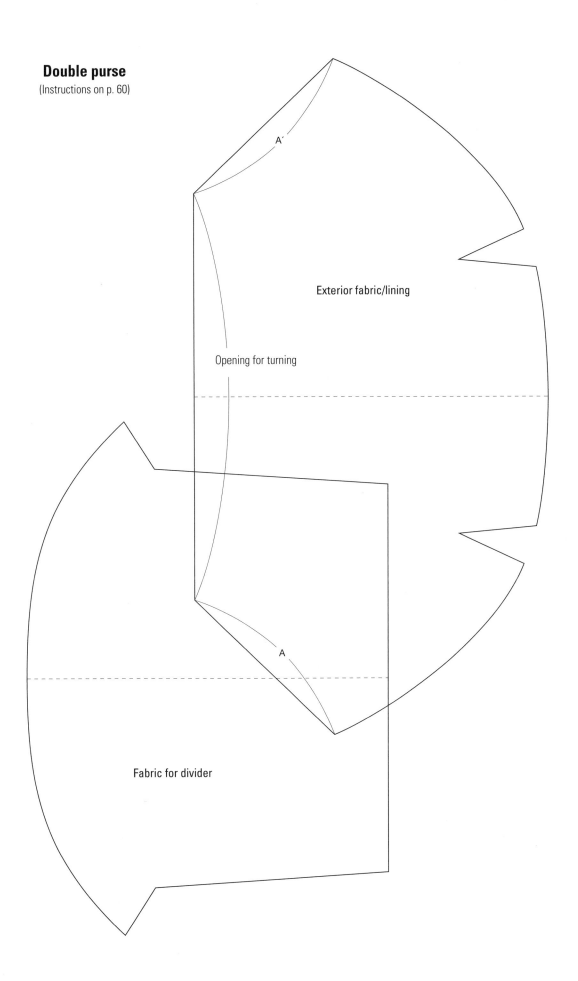

A´

Exterior fabric/lining

Opening for turning

Fabric for divider

A

Business card case

(Instructions on p. 62)

Exterior fabric/pasteboard

Lining

Fabric for pocket partition

Board for pocket partition

Coasters

(Instructions on p. 66)

Right side

Opening for turning

Wrong side

Vanity case

(Instructions on p. 68)

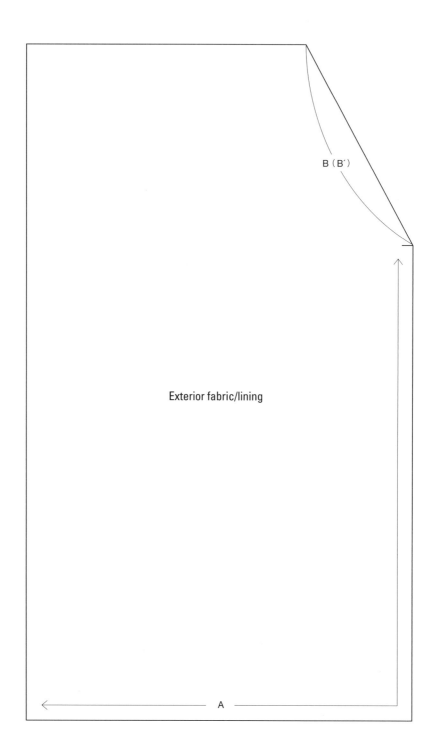

B（B′）

Exterior fabric/lining

A

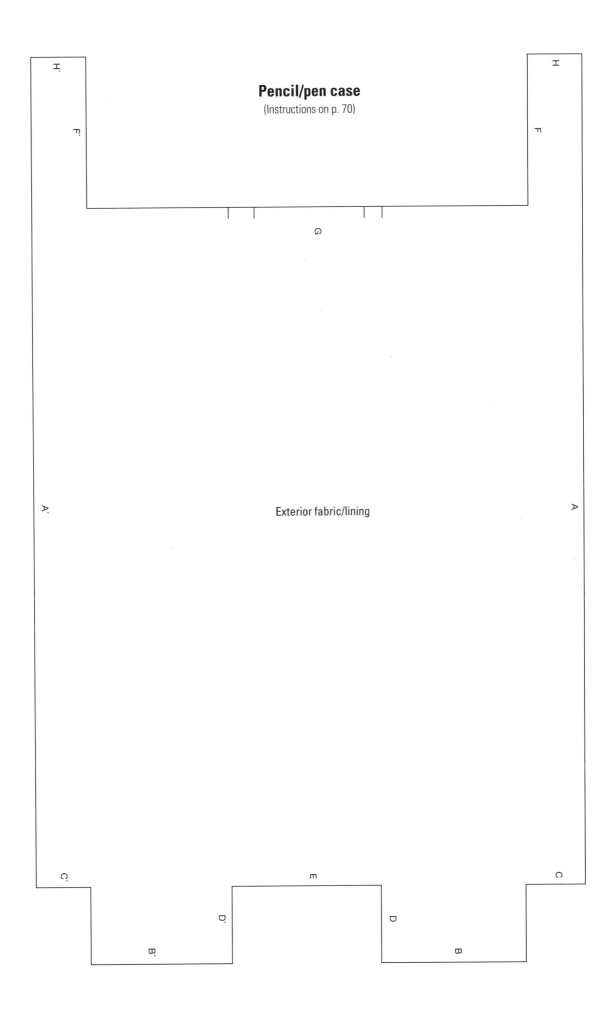

Pencil/pen case

(Instructions on p. 70)

Exterior fabric/lining

Little bird bag

(Instructions on p. 76)

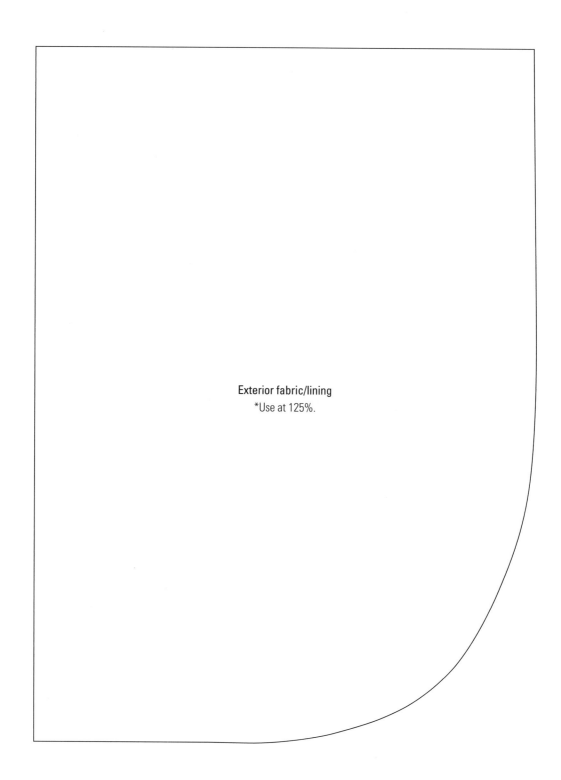

Exterior fabric/lining
*Use at 125%.

Party purse with chain

(Instructions on p. 78)

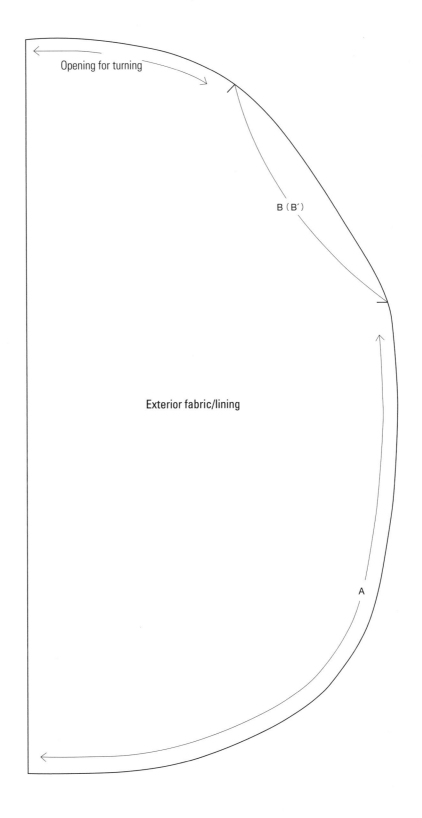

Opening for turning

B (B′)

Exterior fabric/lining

A

City bag
(Instructions on p. 81)

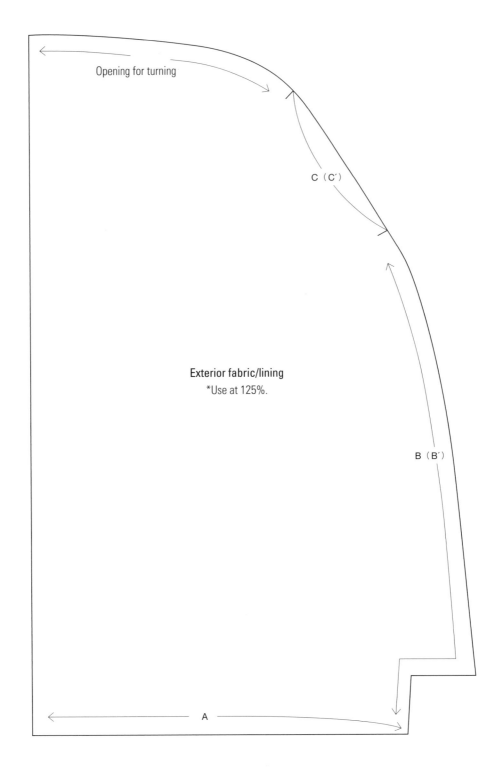

Opening for turning

C（C´）

Exterior fabric/lining
*Use at 125%.

B（B´）

A

Where to find fabric and equipment

Fabric stores

Many of these stores also sell parts, tools and notions for making bags and other accessories

AH! KIMONO	ahkimono.com
Atomic Textiles	vintagefabrix.com
Clothaholics	clothaholics.com
Donna Flower	donnaflower.com
Funky Fabrix	funkyfabrix.com.au
Kimo YES	kimoyes.com
Kimono House	kimonohouse.com.au
Kyoto Kimono	kyotokimono.com
Primrose Design	primrosedesign.com
Retro Age	vintagefabrics.com.au
Retrodepot	reprodepot.com
Revival Fabrics	revivalfabrics.com
Sanshi: Fabric and Fibres from Japan	sanshi.com.au
Vintage Fabric Market	vintagefabricmarket.co.uk
Vintage Pretty	vintagepretty.com
Yokodana	yokodana.com
Ziguzagu Fabrics	ziguzagu.net

Parts, tools, notions

Buttonmania	buttonmania.com.au
Catherine's Place	catherinesplace.com.au
Nicole Mallalieu Design	nicolemdesign.com.au
Puddle Crafts	puddlecrafts.co.uk
Studio Mio	studiomio.com.au
Tall Poppy Craft	tallpoppycraft.com
The Button Bower	thebuttonbower.com
U-handbag	u-handbag.com
Vintage Buttons	vintagebuttons.net

Useful bag templates

Clover	clover-usa.com

See 'Florida Tote Collection' and 'Trace 'N Create Bag Templates'

General craft resource

Etsy	etsy.com

For countless independent stores selling vintage fabric, buttons, notions, bag making accessories and more.

Author's biography

Kaoru Ishikawa (sova*)

Following studies in architecture, interior and furniture design, Ishikawa taught herself bag making. She currently designs and produces bags and other small items using old kimono and western-pattern vintage fabrics under the business name 'sova*'. The name means owl, her favourite bird, in Czech. Enchanted by the interesting quality and texture of old textiles and the never-fading beauty of their colours and modern patterns, Ishikawa pursues the creation of items that are easy to use in everyday life, under the concept 'cherishing the old, creating the new'. She wishes to be close to people and to make things that make them happy.

Vintage Fabric Accessories:
Stylish creations from recycled fabrics

First designed and published in Japan in 2009
by Graphic-sha Publishing Co., Ltd.
1-14-17 Kudan-kita, Chiyoda-ku,
Tokyo 102-0073 Japan

Copyright © 2009 Kaoru Ishikawa (sova*)
Copyright © 2009 Graphic-sha Publishing Co., Ltd.

English edition published in Australia in 2010 by
The Images Publishing Group Pty Ltd
ABN 89 059 734 431
6 Bastow Place, Mulgrave, Victoria 3170, Australia
Tel: +61 3 9561 5544 Fax: +61 3 9561 4860
books@imagespublishing.com
www.imagespublishing.com

Copyright © The Images Publishing Group Pty Ltd 2010
The Images Publishing Group Reference Number: 934

National Library of Australia Cataloguing-in-Publication entry:

Author:	Ishikawa, Kaoru.
Title:	Vintage fabric accessories : stylish creations from recycled fabrics / by Kaoru Ishikawa.
ISBN	9781864704099 (pbk.)
Edition:	1st ed.
Subjects:	Dress accessories.
	Handicraft.
Dewey Number:	646.48

IMAGES has included on its website a page for special notices in relation to this and our other publications.
Please visit www.imagespublishing.com.

Staff

Book design and pattern tracing:	Yoshiko Takaki, Katsuki Taguri
Photography:	Ayako Kaneko
Styling:	Kaori Miyama
Illustration:	Yuki Hanashima
Models:	Sharen Ichiba (Space craft), Kaori Kumagai
Hair and makeup:	Kaname Watanabe (HELVETICA hair)
Editing:	Naoko Yamamoto (Graphic-sha Publishing Co., Ltd.)

English edition

Layout:	Shinichi Ishioka
English translation:	Hedges Design Plus
Production:	Kumiko Sakamoto (Graphic-sha Publishing Co., Ltd.)
Editor:	Beth Browne (Images Publishing)

Collaboration
Ribbons: MOKUBA (Handles for bags and purses on pp. 19, 20, 21, 22, 23 and 30)
Costumes: Tres cotton (pp. 2, p. 15 and p.18)
Glassware: Awabees (Glasses on p. 8 and a glass jar on p. 34)

Printed in China by: Everbest Printing Co., Ltd.